No One Asks to be Born...

The Endless Enigma of Reality: Resolved.

By

Patti Markow

PUbLiC ApOLOgy:

Public apology is hereby made to Wal-mart Stores Incorporated for any misconstruction of the words of this book that might imply that Wal-mart is guilty of any wrong-doing. I am a regular customer of Wal-mart and the inspiration was realized upon one day walking into a Wal-mart store. This book is more intended to bring to light a "bug" in the general commercial entity establishment rules and regulations, as they may apply to the employment of Human Resources, Wal-mart Stores not being excluded but certainly not KNOWINGLY in commit of ANY crime and certainly not the only entity this unrealized "bug" does, may or could affect upon passage of appropriate legislation and provided all due commercial entity consideration is given.

This book is dedicated to
ALL people, With adoration
and all due respect.

No One Asks to be Born...

By Patti Markow

CHapter ONe:

I spent many years of my life trying to resolve the endless enigma that would make some sense of life's purpose. I thought that if I applied all of my mental powers I would be able to come up with something that might save the world from what seemed to be an impending or perpetual doom.

Meanwhile, the quality of my life was no more than that which could be afforded by a below poverty level, Government funded disability income. It seemed no matter what I might attempt to try, nothing would ever improve that condition well enough to render to me a "good" life for the rest of my life.

I don't want much in life. Just enough to be able to live comfortably, without always having to rely on my family's and the Government's generosity, or getting deep in dept from the use of credit. I concluded that there is no solution to at least once aspect of the endless enigma - that which relates to spirituality. I wrote this:

"No one asks to be born. If you spend your life searching for some spiritual meaning as to why your birth happened, or some deeper meaning to life and existence in general, you are just wasting your time. You are simply the product of your parents' lust. That's the reality of it. You can believe whatever you want to believe, but at the same time, you have to take responsibility for yourself. You cannot just do nothing and live your life expecting sudden good fortune or just live day to day off the charity of the Government and other people. There is no justification to living on the street, a stray human, begging sympathy. No one owes you anything and God is not going to save you."

So the next step in improving my situation was to try to figure out exactly what was involved in one taking responsibility for oneself. Generically, it meant that I must find a way to earn enough money to live the rest of my life without a real or necessary want for anything. At the root of this, I concluded that life is a grande competition and in order to truly be able to afford a decent life, you have to be a winner. I wrote the truth:

"Most people are not born with exceptional good looks, exceptional intelligence or any exceptional talent that can be exploited, making them some kind of celebrity. Most people live at or more toward the bottom of the social and financial pyramid than at the top. There is a competition going on. Some people were born with the quality of looks, intelligence and/or talent that permits them to compete well and live comfortable lives. The majority of people were not born with any exceptional winning capabilities and, unfortunately, there is no apparent, viable option available for those who choose not to compete, or, for whatever reason, cannot compete.

As the current structure continues to make millionaires and billionaires of a few, keeping the rest comparatively poorer or poverty stricken, more and more people become depressed. Many people work very hard at menial jobs their entire lives with nothing to show for it. More people now, than ever, give up after minor effort, searching for some excuse to qualify for free assistance. Or they don't bother trying at all, because free assistance is available.

Many people believe they are 'helping' the problem by making donations to churches and charities when in fact they are just fueling the fire (or justifying a tax deduction). Letting people live off of charity (and yes, often take advantage of charity) does nothing to encourage them to get involved in life and take responsibility for themselves. It encourages them to 'do nothing' or 'do as little as possible' longer. We need a solution that will get people moving and participating cooperatively in life, leading to a healthier economy and greater self-esteem, healthier goals and improved attitudes for everyone."

I had already come to the conclusion that to do nothing, or very little, and rely on charity or the Government to fill the monetary slack in your life was wrong. That would not constitute "taking responsibility" for yourself. So, at least one way, and the most apparent possible way, to make money, and possibly a lot of money, is to be a winner of some sort of competition.

I am 61 years old, disabled and have been out of the competitive workforce for at least 25 years. Being absolutely honest with myself, I just cannot muster the desire or youthful energy to whole-heartedly enter into a competition anymore. But I do want to take responsibility for myself.

I started thinking about this grande competition which is life. It is the cause of the attitude so many people have adopted - a lack of spirit. There are always more losers than there are winners. It is very depressing and disheartening to be a loser. But why should that be the case at all? And medicating these "depressed" people is not a solution, either.

I wrote the following:

"You should not have to compete to live. You should be able to cooperate in life, with whatever your abilities and disabilities, and have a good life in return."

That is a state of reality that just does not exist.

Without the energy to try to compete in the workplace anymore, I had to find another way to make money. "Winning a competition" was a means to an end that was on my list, but not in a preferred position. I thought I could try to earn money on my own and turned to the internet.

Chapter Two:

It does not take much time or deep searching to find all kinds of programs being offered on the internet that proclaim they will make you an overnight millionaire WITHOUT competition. That seemed enticing enough, so I started checking them out. I could not check ALL of them out because there are probably a million or more of them. But I purchased access, learned what they were about and then received refunds for enough of them to give me the general idea.

Those that were not outright scams all had something in common. They were all about a glitch that was found somewhere in the ever-developing world of internet commerce, exploiting that glitch and cashing in.

I have no doubt that at least some of these "hackers" probably made millions exploiting the glitches that they found. But by the time they put together a marketable program to teach others how to exploit the same glitch, the business that owned the operation that contained the "bug" became aware of the bug themselves and corrected it. The programs that the hackers were marketing, in an effort to cash in more on their "miracle discovery," no longer worked.

At least, after all of my searching, trial and error, I learned two more possible ways to make money, and possibly a lot of money:

1. Run a scam;
2. Exploit something.

Well, running a scam is usually illegal and I did not want to have anything to do with that. That was not a honest way to take responsibility for myself. To exploit something is alright, if it is yourself you are exploiting (like a celebrity exploiting his own talent) or you give permission for someone else to exploit something about you. But if it is something else you want to exploit, something that belongs to someone else or you don't have the permission to exploit, that also seems dishonest, if not outright illegal.

I took a deep breath and sighed. I got dressed and thought that resorting to the non-preference of competition was really the only alternative. I did not want to put a lot of brains and energy into it, but I would put in an application to become a cashier at Wal-mart. Applying for that type of position is not HIGHLY competitive, you were not required to "dress for success" or "play games that mother never taught you" (corporate games), and they paid a salary: probably minimum wage. I felt myself succumbing to a subtle depression, doomed to never having a self-sufficient, comfortable life of not wanting or needing for anything I could not afford. Whether I liked that destiny or not, it appeared at this point that I would never be able to exist without having to rely on the generosity of my family, assistance from the Government and credit cards.   As unhappy and unwilling as I was, I had to face it.

As I walked into Wal-mart, I stopped for a bit and looked at the cashiers. They were all human beings, cooperating with life: they were working and trying to earn a living for themselves. They were making an honest effort to take responsibility for themselves. But what was truly the return for all their effort? Never-ending struggle and probably misery. What a sad state. They were not receiving a "good" life in return for their cooperation, with whatever their abilities or disabilities.

I decided to cancel my job application and return to trying to figure out this endless enigma - but not as it relates to spirituality, as it relates to reality.

I did not want to live the rest of my life off of the pittance I receive by the grace of the Government. I wanted money. I wanted enough money to at least be able to afford a "good" life. I did not ever expect to achieve billionaire status, but I could fathom no logic to thinking that I could not drastically improve my living situation - or why SO MANY PEOPLE like me, who are willing to cooperate in life and take responsibility for themselves, seem doomed to a life of financial struggles.

Putting my thinking cap back on, I reviewed what I had thus far determined as the possible means to a more desirable end to my financial dilemma. There are 3 ways to make a lot of money: win a competition, run a scam or exploit something.

Winning a competition is down right hard. Running a scam is usually illegal. Having to exploit something, as the only option left, does not seem like a right and honest way to make money, unless your are only exploiting yourself, something you own or something you have permission to exploit.

I thought about Wal-mart. At one end you have the lowly cashiers and other positions that represent the low, minimum or near minimum wage earners. But at the other end you have the billionaire Walton family.

The Walton family did not win a competition to achieve their wealth. They are the stockholders of a corporation. The corporation is not a scam. So what's left? Something has to be being exploited, dishonestly, unethically or illegally, since the Walton family is certainly not exploiting itself. It had to be those lowly cashiers and other minimum-wagers who were being exploited, although if there were something dishonest or illegal about it, it is not obvious or recognized as such or it would have been detected long before now.

I gave that line of thought more consideration. I related it to ALL commercial entities, where the owners and/or stockholders receive the benefit of the bulk profits earned, thanks to the efforts of the entity's employees: the human resources. Could there possibly be something to the idea that possibly ALL of any commercial entity's employees are somehow being exploited, since it is the owners and/or stockholders that typically make a lot of money and not the typical employee? And do commercial entities really HAVE PERMISSION to exploit these people?

Competition, scam or exploitation. I narrowed it down to those being the only possibilities. It had to be one of them.

Chapter Three:

I took a deep breath and sighed in an effort to put together some logical thought on the matter.

Okay. There is competition for the various jobs within a commercial entity. The better qualified win the competition and receive the higher rate of regular compensation. But competition for jobs has nothing to do with the owners and stockholders earning profits. The owners and/or stockholders are not winning any kind of competition by owning the entity or holding shares of stock, even though it could be said that a commercial entity competes successfully in the free market if it earns a profit. We can eliminate the possibility that the owners and/or stockholders are running some kind of scam. It HAD TO BE exploitation.

Somehow, the owners and/or stockholders of commercial entities are making a lot of money from the exploitation of the commercial entity's human resources and getting away with it. It had to be.   And since it is not themselves they are exploiting, and they CANNOT SAY that they OWN the human resources that are being exploited: that would constitute claiming ownership of human beings (slavery), there has to be something dishonest, unethical or illegal going on. It HAS to be. I truly doubt that anyone would consciously grant permission to let themselves be exploited "like" a slave if they were fully aware that is the implication of their "employment agreement."

I worked on the problem long and hard, creating simplified examples and diagrams for myself so that I could get to the problem's core, and I believe I have found it. I have found the "glitch" in the "commercial entity" that is being exploited to make the Walton family, and other similar, stockholding people, billionaires while keeping the majority of the entity's human resources financially struggling.

The owners and/or stockholders of today's typical commercial entities ARE claiming an indirect type of OWNERSHIP of the entities HUMAN resources. Although human resources do not currently appear on a commercial entity's balance sheet as an asset owned, but rather an expense and liability, any commercial entity would have to agree that the entity's most valuable "asset" is, in fact, its human resources. Direct ownership of human resources may not be documented, thereby quasi-protecting the entity from making a public declaration or acknowledgment of the ownership of "slaves." However, it is no secret that anything that may result from what human resources expends its energy on, during working hours,

IS owned by the entity. So, indirectly, by claiming ownership of the energy expelled by human resources and the resultant value that the human energy adds to the entity, translatable into dollars and cents, the entity IS claiming a type of ownership of the human resources: the human beings that the human profit-making energy is attributable to.

As a result of non-declaration of human resources as the entity's profit generating asset, a commercial entity legally DOES CLAIM OWNERSHIP of 100% of the net profits generated by its human resources without just consideration to the fact that the human resources IS HUMAN and possibly entitled to just and fair share of the net profits its human energy is responsible for generating. This is, more or less, a constitution of human EXPLOITATION. In fact, a typical commercial entity would generate zero to very little profits at all if it WERE NOT for its human resources. And in many cases, the commercial entity compensates the human resources as lowly as competitively possible, staking a claim on the profit-making human resource energy in a manner that will generate the highest possible profits.

There is only ONE WAY that this would not truly be like the ownership of SLAVES, and that is if the employees are compensated fully for the full and actual value of what their work is worth: a percentage of the commercial entity's net profits, determined by the percentage of the value of the entity that is attributable to human resources. This percentage of the net profits should distributed to the HUMAN employees, equally, IN ADDITION TO their "competed for," regular compensation for the jobs they perform. This percentage of the net profits rightfully BELONGS TO the HUMAN RESOURCES that gave the profit power to the otherwise inanimate corporation and NOT solely to the owners and/or stockholders of the business.

If it is implicated by a commercial

entity's "employment agreement" that this percentage of the profits is a non-entitlement, in whatever the fancy words that are composed, then the employment agreement is veritably nothing more than a scam that enables the corporation to hire human resources into naught but slave labor.

CHapter Four:

All of my thought and analysis of the problem led me to a conclusion that formulated a legal argument:

"It is ILLEGAL for the owner(s) of any commercial entity, including any business or corporation, that employs HUMAN RESOURCES to in ANY WAY, actual OR implied, claim OWNERSHIP of that percentage of the entity's value (prior tangible assets + net income) that is attributable to human resources. "Implied" would include the claim of any sole right to reap the benefit(s) of that value. That would constitute a direct or indirect OWNERSHIP of HUMAN BEINGS by claiming sole ownership of the value generated by the human energy of the human resources.

In order that the employment of human resources NOT be constituted or construed as HUMAN EXPLOITATION, a percentage of the NET PROFITS, equal to the percentage of the entity's value (prior tangible assets + net income) that is attributable to human resources, MUST BE distributed to those HUMAN EMPLOYEES that ARE the entity's 'asset:' Human Resources. This percentage of the net profits must be distributed to the human resources IN ADDITION TO the employee's agreed upon 'rate of regular compensation' and NOT claimed as belonging exclusively to the owner(s) of the entity.

The agreed upon 'rate of regular compensation' must only be construed to be the equivalent of a 'contract retainer,' assuring the entity that the associated job will in fact be performed, REGARDLESS of the amount of any profits that may be earned by the entity, and NOT as the final 'fixed and full' amount of compensation owed to and earned by the human resources. Human resources MUST be compensated the full and actual dollar amount that their work is worth, as determined by the percentage of the net profits that is equal to the percentage of the value (prior tangible assets + net income) of the entity that is attributable to human resources."

If all of a commercial entity's employees, regardless of position of employment and amount of regular compensation (which depends on the difficulty of the job being performed), do not receive an equal and fair share of the profits they worked to generate for a corporation, then in reality they are nothing more than exploited slaves owned and traded by the commercial entity's owners and/or stockholders, collectively, under the guise of the legal "person" (slave) entity which is named the commercial establishment. There has to be an end to veritable slave empires and the demand that a fair share of commercial entity's profits rightfully belong to the people who worked to generate the profits and not all of the profits only to benefit the entity's owners and holders of the paper "shares" of stock.

The owners of a commercial entity can own the physical, non-human assets of a commercial entity, but when human resources come into play, human resources should not be just considered an expense and liability of that ownership. Stockholders can receive a share of the profits as a return for the capital they invested and they can hold an ownership of physical, non-human assets - real estate, equipment, etc. - which they can sell should the corporation dissolve. They cannot in any way, directly or indirectly, claim an ownership of the entity's human resources OR sole right and ownership of the portion of the value (prior tangible assets + net income) of the commercial entity that is attributable to human resources.

The non-human assets of a commercial entity typically do not earn the profits. It is the employees that give the profit-yielding life to the commercial entity: the human resources. If the human resources of an entity are not to be veritably owned and exploited like slaves , then a fair share of the entity's net profits rightfully belong to them. And all jobs, from CEO to the minimum wage earner, should be considered as equally important roles that had to be played in order to earn the entity's profits. So although the CEO might earn a higher rate of regular compensation due to the increased difficulty and responsibility associated with his job, when it comes to profit sharing all employees - top to bottom - should receive an equal and fair share of the percentage that belongs to them.

If the jobs performed within a commercial entity are performed by non-humans, such as machines or robots, then the owners and/or stockholders claiming ownership of the profit-making resource is legitimate and legal. But when the jobs are performed by HUMAN BEINGS, that should be considered as something completely different and claiming ANY KIND of ownership is truly against the laws of Human Rights, even if the ownership is only of the human energy expelled and the dollar increase in the entity's worth caused by that energy.

The unique quality of energy and productivity that human resources contributes to a commercial entity is truly not compensated as if it is special and extremely valuable. In fact, the current minimum wage is evidence that HUMAN energy and productivity is not considered very valuable at all.

Minimum wage is an insult to how precious human energy and productivity is. It is sad to think that we put more value on gemstones and their making than we do on the precious and special qualities that human beings are able to add to the otherwise inanimate (and non-profitable) commercial entity. There is really no price that can be placed on the value of human energy and productivity - not because it is worthless, but because it is incomparable.

Human resources is truly the most valuable "asset" of a commercial entity and the everyday people that compose the human resources should be compensated as such. Why must an individual be an "injured party" before any kind of substantial value is given to his/her energy and productivity and a non-injured party be considered as worth only minimum wage?

In fact, if human resources energy and productivity constitutes and/or generates 74% to 96% of any commercial entity's value, then 74% to 96% of the corporation's net profits belong to the employees...not the owners and/or stockholders.

Let's use an example:

Sam & Joe establish a corporation called "Lawn Cutters" and buy a lawn mower for $225. Sam & Joe don't want to cut lawns themselves, so the lawn mower just sits there, depreciating. The value (prior tangible assets + net income) of the corporation is a depreciating $225.

Sam & Joe decide to hire Ralph for $10/hr. to do the lawn cutting and plan to charge $60 for every lawn that is cut. Ralph uses the company lawn mower. In one day, 8 hours, Ralph cuts 5 lawns and earns $300 for the company.

Out of the money earned, the "overhead" is deducted: $80 for Ralph's salary and let's allow $10 for depreciation of the lawn mower. The total net profit was $210. Now the value of the corporation is $225 (lawn mower - prior tangible asset) plus $210 (net profit): $435.00.

The $210 is the value added to the corporation by the HUMAN RESOURCES (Ralph). $210 represents 48.27% of the corporation's value that Sam & Joe should not LEGALLY be able to claim ownership of: it's directly attributable and caused by the energy of the corporation's HUMAN resources. That means 48.27% of the net profits they ALSO should not be able to claim ownership of: it belongs to the human resource. So Ralph should get an additional

$101.37, which is 48.27% of the net profits.

Sam & Joe just made $108.63 from the depreciating lawn mower that they own and as a return for their contribution of ingenuity and capital. Ralph made $181.37, certainly a better day's earnings than just his salary of $80 and the TRUE VALUE of what his work was worth. Sam & Joe are happy. Ralph is happy. And it was all done fairly and ethically.

The way commercial entities operate now, Sam & Joe would earn $210 from their depreciating lawn mower and Ralph would earn only his $80. Ralph put in the time, sweat and energy - the HUMAN RESOURCE that added the profit power to the corporation - and he is veritably exploited like a slave or was scammed into slave labor as a result of some employment agreement. Ralph does not receive the true and actual dollar value that the work he performed is worth.

Although not Sam, Joe NOR Ralph could possibly know the true and actual value of Ralph's work until after the net profits are calculated and the new value of the entity has been determined, Ralph could have been compensated. Instead, Sam and Joe keep 100% of the net profits. That is truly dishonest, unfair and SHOULD BE illegal. All Sam & Joe did was buy a depreciating lawn mower, invest capital and organize a corporation.

It is illegal to own, exploit and trade human beings. Yet that's veritably what current owners and/or stockholders of today's commercial entities are doing. Veritable slave empires have made stockholders billionaires, while the people who do the actual work are typically struggling because they do not receive their rightful due - the true dollar value of what their work is worth to any commercial entity. It is not logical, honest or ethical and it seems to be a gross violation of human rights, but that's what is going on.

CHapter Five:

There you have it. The endless enigma of reality is resolved. Passage of legislation to rectify the current entity/employee situation would not only greatly improve the financial well being of America's employees, but also have an incredibly positive affect on our Nation's economy.

So as I was meditating upon the reality which constitutes the current system of life...to find what must be the "bug," or "unintentional error," in the logic that ANY HUMAN BEING, regardless of innate, acquired or accidental abilities and/or disabilities, should be literally "doomed" to a life of financial troubles and hardships, my concluded thoughts generated a legal argument that relates to employment, business and human rights law.

Although I believe my argument is valid, I am not a lawyer. The issues it involves must be debated by knowledgeable legal minds in order to confirm the validity. Should it be determined that the argument is valid, the introduction of legislation would be necessary in order to clarify in the law the extended words that would insure true and just respect of an individual's human rights, specifically as they relate to employment and the illegality in the exploitation of a commercial entity's human resources.

It would take cooperation of America's commercial entities to voluntarily correct this flaw in the current system, which would be a miraculous turn of events and situations for America's employees. But, unfortunately, it will probably require at least one major class action lawsuit against a major entity to get the attention of the public and possibly, if necessary, the Supreme Court.

The publication of this book is a sincere effort bring to light the "bug" and/or "error" that leaves SO MANY HONEST AND COOPERATIVE individuals "doomed" to an inappropriate life of financial struggles, hardship and possibly poverty when it should be INSURED by the laws of this great country that NO ONE'S HUMAN RIGHTS will in any way be violated.